Game Theory & Behavioral Economics: The Basics of Behavioral Game Theory

Roggie Clark

Continue Learning At Our Website: Roggieclarkbooks.com

Continue exploring educational resources, tools, books, workbooks, and learning materials designed to help readers continue building knowledge and practical skills. Visit: www.roggieclarkbooks.com

Inside you'll find:

- Educational worksheets
- Beginner-friendly guides
- Printable activities
- Companion materials for books and courses

A growing library of educational content for readers, collectors, learners, parents, teachers, and lifelong students.

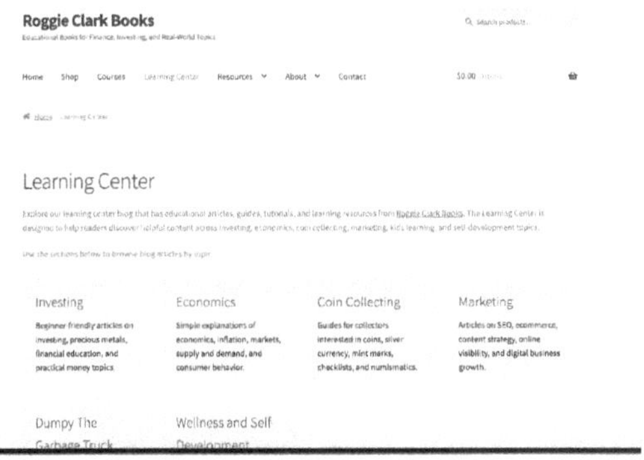

The Strategic Guide to U.S. Mint Gold and Silver Coin Investing

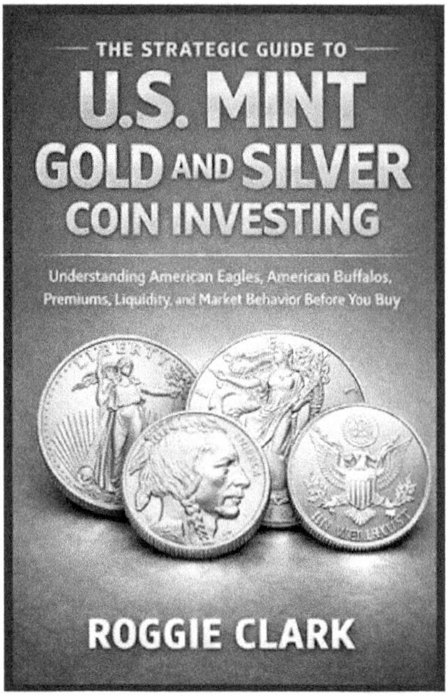

Rather than offering a general introduction to precious metals, this guide examines how American Gold Eagles, American Gold Buffalos, and Silver American Eagles behave in real investor markets.

https://www.amazon.com/Strategic-Guide-U-S-Silver-Investing/dp/B0GQKJF9K6

Copyright

Title: Game theory & behavioral economics: The basics of behavioral game theory
Author: Roggie Clark

Cover Design: Roggie Clark
Editing: Renee' Clark

Printed in the United States of America

Disclaimer

The views and opinions expressed in this publication are those of the author and do not necessarily reflect the official policies, positions, opinions, or viewpoints of any individual, company, organization, institution, agency, or entity referenced or mentioned within this work.

The author is not necessarily affiliated with, endorsed by, sponsored by, or compensated by any individuals, companies, organizations, brands, institutions, products, or services referenced within this publication unless specifically stated otherwise. Any examples, sample situations, stories, illustrations, or scenarios presented may be fictionalized or simplified for educational purposes. Any resemblance to actual persons, living or dead, businesses, or events is purely coincidental unless otherwise stated.

The information, ideas, strategies, concepts, techniques, opinions, suggestions, and educational materials contained in this publication are provided on an "as is" basis without warranties of any kind, either express or implied. While every effort has been made to provide accurate and current information, neither the author nor the publisher makes any representations or warranties regarding the completeness, accuracy, reliability, suitability, or applicability of the information presented.

This publication is intended solely for educational and informational purposes and should not be interpreted as professional advice of any kind, including but not limited to financial, investment, legal, tax, business, medical, mental health, educational, psychological, or other professional guidance. Readers should conduct their own independent research and consult appropriately qualified professionals before making decisions that may affect their finances, health, business, education, legal matters, personal circumstances, or other important areas of life.

Results, outcomes, and experiences may vary significantly among individuals. Neither the author nor the publisher guarantees any specific outcomes, results, earnings, performance improvements, personal achievements, or benefits resulting from the use of information contained in this publication.

By reading, accessing, or using this publication, you acknowledge and agree that the author and publisher shall not be held liable for any direct, indirect, incidental, consequential, financial, personal, emotional, or other damages, losses, or claims arising from the use, misuse, interpretation, or application of information contained within this publication. You assume full responsibility for any actions, decisions, and outcomes resulting from the use of this material.

Image Credits and Public Domain Notice

All images, illustrations, graphics, photographs, visual references, and related materials included in this publication are believed to be in the public domain, used under applicable licenses or permissions, created by the author or publisher, or obtained from sources that clearly identify them as available for lawful use.

The author and publisher have made a good faith effort to use only visual materials that are lawfully available for use and distribution. Where applicable, images and visual materials may have been resized, cropped, edited, enhanced, stylized, modified, reformatted, or arranged for educational, informational, design, formatting, or presentation purposes.

This publication is intended for educational, informational, and illustrative purposes only. The inclusion of any image, artwork, photograph, visual reference, symbol, historical material, design, or graphic element is not intended to claim ownership over public domain materials or any third-party intellectual property rights that remain with their respective owners.

If you believe any image or visual material included in this publication has been used in error, please contact the author or publisher so the matter may be reviewed and corrected in future editions or releases if necessary.

Any factual information, specifications, historical references, values, descriptions, statistics, or related content accompanying visual materials are provided for general informational purposes only and may change over time. Readers should conduct their own independent research and consult appropriate sources or qualified professionals when making decisions based on information presented in this publication.

This publication is independently produced and is not affiliated with, endorsed by, sponsored by, or associated with any company, organization, government agency, institution, trademark holder, or third party unless specifically stated otherwise.

Table of Contents

Introduction: When Your Decisions Depend on Other People

Economics is often described as the study of choices. People decide what to buy, businesses decide what to produce, investors decide where to put their money, and governments decide how to allocate resources. But many of the most important economic choices have another layer: **your outcome depends not only on what you decide, but also on what someone else decides**. A business considering a price reduction has to think about how competitors may respond. A worker negotiating a salary has to consider what an employer may accept. Two companies entering the same market must anticipate each other's strategies. Even something as ordinary as deciding whether to cooperate with another person can depend on whether you believe that person will cooperate with you. These situations introduce us to **game theory**, and once we recognize that the people making these decisions do not always behave exactly as traditional economic models predict, we begin moving into **behavioral game theory**.

What Game Theory Is Really About

Game theory is a framework for studying situations in which two or more decision makers interact strategically. The word "game" can make the subject sound recreational, but a game in economics can represent a serious decision involving businesses, governments, consumers, investors, coworkers, competitors, or virtually anyone whose choices affect another person's outcome.

The individuals or organizations making decisions are generally called **players**. Each player has possible actions or **strategies**, and those strategies can lead to different **payoffs** depending on what everyone involved chooses.

Consider two businesses competing in the same market. Business A is considering lowering its price. If it lowers the price while Business B maintains its current price, Business A may attract some of Business B's customers. That sounds like an easy decision.

But what happens if Business B lowers its price too?

Now both businesses may earn less money without either gaining much of an advantage.

This is where the strategic nature of the decision becomes important. Business A cannot properly evaluate its choice by asking only:

"What happens if I lower my price?"

It also has to ask:

"What is Business B likely to do if I lower my price?"

And Business B is probably thinking about Business A in much the same way.

This interdependence is at the heart of game theory. The best decision for one player can depend on the decisions available to another player, what each player knows, what each player wants, and what each player expects the other to do.

Game theory gives us a structured way to examine these situations.

Some games involve direct competition. Others involve opportunities for cooperation. Some occur once, while others happen repeatedly. Players may have complete information about the situation, or they may have to make decisions while dealing with uncertainty.

The framework becomes particularly useful because strategic interaction appears throughout economics.

Businesses respond to competitors' prices. Countries respond to one another's trade policies. Buyers and sellers negotiate. Employers and employees bargain. Firms decide whether to enter markets where competitors are already operating. Consumers may even change their behavior based on what they see other consumers doing.

In each case, there is more happening than an isolated choice.

There is a choice being made **in response to the possibility of another choice**.

That distinction is essential to understanding the rest of this book.

From Traditional Game Theory to Behavioral Game Theory

Traditional game theory gives economists a powerful way to model strategic decisions. However, like many economic models, it often begins with assumptions about rational behavior.

A rational player is generally expected to evaluate available strategies, consider the resulting payoffs, and choose an action that best advances their interests given the circumstances of the game.

This assumption is useful because economic models need structure. If we assumed that everyone behaved completely randomly, predicting strategic behavior would become nearly impossible.

But people are not random, nor are they perfectly calculating.

Suppose two people are dividing $100. One person proposes keeping $90 and giving the other person $10. If rejecting the proposal means both people receive nothing, a narrow monetary interpretation might suggest that the second person should accept the $10. Ten dollars is financially better than zero.

Yet the second person might reject the offer.

Why?

Perhaps the division feels unfair. Perhaps accepting it feels like rewarding the other person's selfishness. Perhaps the person is willing to sacrifice $10 to punish behavior they dislike.

From a purely monetary perspective, rejecting the offer may initially appear difficult to explain. From a behavioral perspective, however, the decision becomes much more interesting.

The person's payoff may involve more than money.

Behavioral economics examines how psychological, social, emotional, and cognitive factors influence economic choices. It challenges the idea that human decision making can always be understood through perfectly rational optimization alone.

Bring behavioral economics together with game theory, and we arrive at **behavioral game theory**.

Behavioral game theory examines strategic decisions while paying closer attention to how people actually behave. It allows us to ask whether real players consistently follow the strategies predicted by traditional models and, when they do not, what may explain the difference.

Fairness may matter.

Trust may matter.

Reputation may matter.

Losses may feel different from equivalent gains.

A person's expectations about another player's intentions may affect how they respond.

People may cooperate even when immediate self-interest suggests otherwise. They may punish someone at a cost to themselves. They may make mistakes, misunderstand probabilities, rely on mental shortcuts, or change their behavior after observing what other players have done.

This does not mean traditional game theory becomes useless. Quite the opposite.

Traditional game theory gives us a benchmark. It establishes a structured prediction about strategic behavior. Behavioral game theory allows us to compare those predictions with observed human behavior and explore why differences occur.

That relationship is important.

The goal is not to create a contest between "rational game theory" and "irrational people." Human behavior is more complicated than that.

Sometimes people behave remarkably close to what a traditional model predicts. Sometimes they do not. Experience can change behavior. Incentives can change behavior. Repetition can change behavior. The way a problem is presented can even change behavior.

Behavioral game theory gives us additional tools for understanding those differences.

Why Understanding Strategic Behavior Matters

You do not need to be sitting at a game theory matrix to participate in a strategic interaction. Many decisions in everyday economic life already have the basic characteristics of a game.

Consider negotiation.

If you are negotiating the price of something, you have an amount you would prefer to pay. The seller has an amount they would prefer to receive. Neither side necessarily knows exactly how far the other is willing to move.

Your offer therefore communicates information.

An extremely low offer might save you money if accepted, but it could also cause the seller to believe that reaching an agreement with you is unlikely. A higher offer might improve the probability of an agreement while reducing the financial advantage you hoped to gain.

The seller faces a similar problem.

Both players are choosing strategies while forming expectations about the other.

Competition creates another type of strategic problem.

Imagine two companies considering whether to spend heavily on advertising. If one advertises while the other does not, the advertiser may gain market share. If both advertise aggressively, they may largely cancel out one another's advantage while increasing costs for both companies.

Should either company stop advertising?

Not necessarily.

If one stops while the other continues, the company that stops could lose customers. This means both firms can find themselves maintaining an expensive strategy partly because of what they expect their competitor to do.

Game theory helps us understand the structure of that problem. Behavioral game theory allows us to go further by asking how factors such as overconfidence, fear of losing market share, past rivalry, expectations, and perceptions of competitors might influence the decisions being made.

Cooperation presents another important application.

People frequently have opportunities to benefit by working together, but cooperation can require trust. If you cooperate while the other player takes advantage of you, you may end up worse off. If both sides refuse to cooperate because neither trusts the other, they may also miss an outcome that would have benefited everyone.

This tension between **individual incentives and collective outcomes** will appear repeatedly throughout this book.

Understanding strategic behavior does not give you the ability to perfectly predict what another person will do. That is not the purpose of game theory, and human behavior is far too complex for such a promise.

What these frameworks can give you is a more disciplined way of thinking.

Instead of asking only, "What should I do?" you can begin asking:

What choices are available to the other player?

What incentives influence those choices?

How might they respond to my strategy?

What do they believe I am going to do?

Would our behavior change if we had to interact again?

Is cooperation possible?

What happens if each of us simply follows our own immediate self-interest?

And perhaps most importantly for behavioral game theory: **Are the assumptions I am making about the other person's behavior realistic?**

Those questions can reveal aspects of a decision that are easy to overlook when we think only about our own preferences.

Throughout this book, we will build this framework systematically. We will begin with players, strategies, and payoffs before examining dominant strategies and **Nash Equilibrium**. We will then explore the **Prisoner's Dilemma**, competition, cooperation, and repeated games before bringing behavioral economics more directly into the analysis.

The final goal is not simply to memorize terminology. It is to understand how strategic choices work when the people making those choices are human.

Last Thoughts

Game theory begins with a simple realization: your best decision can depend on what someone else decides to do. Behavioral game theory adds an equally important realization: the person on the other side of that decision may care about more than the outcome a traditional model assumes they should value. People respond to incentives, but they can also respond to fairness, trust, expectations, emotions, previous interactions, and the behavior of others. Understanding both sides gives us a richer framework for studying strategic decision making. In Chapter 1, we will establish that framework by examining the three fundamental pieces of a game: **players, strategies, and payoffs**.

Chapter 1: Players, Strategies, and Payoffs

Game theory becomes easier to analyze once we identify the basic structure of the situation. Regardless of whether we are examining two businesses competing on price, countries negotiating a trade agreement, or individuals deciding whether to cooperate, we can usually begin with three questions: Who is making the decisions? What choices are available to them? What does each participant gain or lose from the possible outcomes? These questions give us the three fundamental components of a game: players, strategies, and payoffs. Understanding how these pieces fit together gives us a foundation for analyzing more complicated strategic situations later in the book.

Understanding Players and Strategic Choices

We introduced players in the previous chapter as the individuals or organizations making decisions within a game. Now we need to examine their role more carefully.

A player does not necessarily have to be a single person. A player could be a company, government, political organization, household, investor, labor union, or another decision-making entity.

What matters is that the player has some ability to choose between different actions and that those choices affect the outcome of the game.

Suppose two coffee shops operate across the street from each other. Both are considering whether to remain open later in the evening.

We could identify them simply as:

- Player A: Coffee Shop A
- Player B: Coffee Shop B

Each business has a decision to make. However, neither decision occurs completely independently.

If Coffee Shop A stays open late while Coffee Shop B closes early, Coffee Shop A may capture most of the evening customers. If both businesses stay open late, they may have to split those customers while both incur the additional cost of remaining open.

If neither stays open late, both avoid the additional operating costs, but both also give up the potential evening revenue.

The important point is that the value of Coffee Shop A's decision depends partly on what Coffee Shop B decides to do.

This is what makes the situation strategic.

A **strategic choice** is a decision made while considering the possible actions or reactions of other players.

This does not mean that every decision involving multiple people should automatically be treated as a game. If your decision has no meaningful effect on another person's decision or outcome, strategic interaction may not be particularly important.

For instance, imagine that you are choosing between two unrelated books to read over the weekend. Unless your choice somehow affects another person's decision, there is probably little reason to use game theory to analyze it.

Now imagine that you and a classmate must choose between two research topics, but your professor has announced that only one student can receive a special research grant for each topic.

The situation changes.

Your preferred topic still matters, but now you may also want to know which topic your classmate is likely to choose.

Your choice has become strategic because another player's decision affects your potential outcome.

This distinction is important because strategic decision making requires us to look beyond our own preferences.

A player may ask:

What do I want?

But they may also need to ask:

What does the other player want?

What choices are available to them?

What are they likely to choose?

What do they think I will choose?

These questions can continue several levels deep. I may think about what you will do, while you are thinking about what I will do, knowing that I am also thinking about what you will do.

Game theory gives us a framework for organizing this otherwise confusing chain of expectations.

Strategies, Payoffs, and Incentives

Once we identify the players, we need to determine what each player can actually do.

A player's available plan of action is called a strategy.

In a simple game, the strategies may be easy to identify.

Suppose two competing businesses must independently decide whether to:

- Maintain their current price
- Lower their price

Each business therefore has two possible strategies.

We can then examine what happens under the different combinations:

- Both maintain their prices.
- Business A lowers its price while Business B maintains its price.
- Business B lowers its price while Business A maintains its price.
- Both lower their prices.

Notice that the outcome is determined by the **combination of strategies**, not simply by the strategy selected by one player.

This is one reason game theory can be different from ordinary decision analysis.

If Business A asks whether lowering its price is profitable, the correct answer may be:

"It depends on what Business B does."

To understand that dependence, we need payoffs.

As introduced earlier, a payoff represents the outcome a player receives from a particular combination of strategies.

Money is an obvious payoff, but payoffs do not have to be measured exclusively in dollars.

A business may care about profit, market share, customer retention, growth, or survival. A government may care about economic growth, national security, political support, or diplomatic relationships. An individual may care about money, time, reputation, fairness, or some combination of these factors.

In formal game theory, numerical values are often assigned to payoffs so that outcomes can be compared.

Consider our two businesses again.

Suppose each company currently earns $100,000 in profit. If one lowers its price while the other does not, the company lowering its price gains customers and earns $120,000, while its competitor falls to $70,000.

If both lower their prices, increased competition reduces their margins and each earns $80,000.

We could organize the outcomes conceptually as follows:

Business A	Business B	A's Payoff	B's Payoff
Maintain	Maintain	$100,000	$100,000
Lower	Maintain	$120,000	$70,000
Maintain	Lower	$70,000	$120,000
Lower	Lower	$80,000	$80,000

This arrangement is commonly represented using a **payoff matrix**, which organizes the possible strategy combinations and the corresponding outcomes for each player.

The matrix helps us see the strategic problem more clearly.

If Business B maintains its price, Business A would prefer to lower its price because $120,000 is better than $100,000.

But Business B can make exactly the same calculation.

If both companies respond to that incentive by lowering their prices, each ends up earning $80,000 rather than the $100,000 each could have earned if both maintained their prices.

This example introduces an important distinction between **individual incentives** and collective outcomes.

What appears attractive from one player's perspective can produce a less desirable result once every player responds to similar incentives.

This is one of the recurring themes of game theory.

It is also why identifying incentives matters.

An **incentive** is something that makes one choice more or less attractive to a player. Payoffs help us represent those incentives because they show how players value different outcomes.

However, we need to be careful when assigning payoffs.

If we assume that a person cares only about money when that person also cares strongly about fairness, our model may incorrectly describe the person's incentives.

Imagine that you and another person complete the same amount of work. You receive $100 while the other person receives $500.

If we represented your payoff only as "$100," we would capture your monetary reward. But we might fail to capture your dissatisfaction with the unequal distribution.

This issue becomes especially important in behavioral game theory.

The mathematics of the game may be perfectly correct while our assumptions about what the players value are incomplete.

Before we conclude that someone behaved irrationally, we should therefore ask whether we accurately represented their payoff in the first place.

How Strategic Interaction Changes Decision Making

Once players, strategies, and payoffs are combined, we can begin examining strategic interaction more systematically.

The central problem is that a player usually wants to select the strategy that produces the most favorable outcome, but the result may depend on choices outside that player's control.

Let's consider a negotiation.

Suppose you are selling a used car and would like to receive $15,000. A potential buyer would prefer to pay $12,000.

If you were making the decision alone, the situation would be straightforward. You would simply choose the price you prefer.

But you cannot force the buyer to accept $15,000.

Likewise, the buyer cannot simply decide to purchase the vehicle for $12,000 without your agreement.

The final outcome depends on the interaction between both sides.

You may lower your asking price because you believe the buyer is willing to walk away. The buyer may increase the offer because they believe another buyer could purchase the car first.

Each player's behavior changes because another player exists.

Information also becomes important.

Suppose the buyer knows that you urgently need to sell the vehicle today, but you do not know that the buyer has this information.

The buyer may make a lower offer because they believe your urgency makes you more likely to accept.

Now suppose you know that the buyer has already spent weeks searching for this exact model.

That information may strengthen your willingness to reject the lower offer.

Neither the car nor the available money has changed. What changed was the strategic environment.

This illustrates why expectations are so important in game theory.

Players make choices based not only on objective outcomes, but also on what they believe about other players.

Those beliefs can be correct or incorrect.

A business may incorrectly assume that a competitor will match a price reduction. An investor may underestimate how other investors will respond to new information. A negotiator may believe the other side is bluffing when they are actually prepared to walk away.

Strategic decisions therefore involve uncertainty about behavior.

Behavioral game theory makes this even more interesting because players may interpret the same strategic situation differently.

Consider two coworkers who must decide whether to contribute additional effort to a shared project.

One person may think:

"If I work harder, we both benefit."

The other may think:

"If I work harder and they don't, I'll be doing their work for them."

The objective situation may be identical for both people, yet their expectations about cooperation can produce different choices.

Past experiences can influence those expectations. So can trust, personality, social norms, and perceptions of fairness.

This is where strategic interaction begins to move beyond simply listing possible choices.

The player has to form some belief about the environment and the people operating within it.

This does not mean that good strategic thinking requires predicting human behavior perfectly. That would be unrealistic.

Instead, game theory encourages us to think conditionally.

If the other player chooses Strategy A, what is my best response?

If they choose Strategy B, what changes?

What strategy would they prefer if I choose A?

Would my choice give them an incentive to change their behavior?

Thinking in this manner prevents us from evaluating decisions as though other players were passive.

Competitors react.

Negotiating partners respond.

Consumers change behavior.

Governments retaliate or cooperate.

People learn.

Once we recognize this, many economic decisions that initially appear simple become strategic problems.

And that brings us toward one of the most important questions in game theory: Is there a strategy that a player would prefer regardless of what the other player does?

If there is, we may have what is known as a dominant strategy.

Last Thoughts

Players, strategies, and payoffs provide the basic language we need to describe a game. Players make choices, strategies represent the actions available to them, and payoffs show how they value the resulting outcomes. But the real power of game theory comes from examining how these components interact. A strategy that looks attractive in isolation may become less attractive once we consider another player's response, and a payoff that appears straightforward may become more complicated when fairness, trust, reputation, or other behavioral factors matter. In the next chapter, we will build on this foundation by examining **dominant strategies** and **Nash Equilibrium**, two concepts that help us identify what players may choose when each person is responding strategically to the choices of others.

Chapter 2: Dominant Strategies and Nash Equilibrium

Once we understand players, strategies, and payoffs, we can begin asking a more difficult question: **Which strategy should a player actually choose?** Sometimes one choice consistently produces a better outcome regardless of what another player does. In other situations, the best choice depends entirely on the strategy selected by someone else. Game theory gives us several ways to analyze these situations, but two of the most important are dominant strategies and Nash Equilibrium. These concepts move us beyond simply describing a game and allow us to examine how players respond to incentives, how strategic outcomes develop, and why a stable outcome is not necessarily the best outcome.

Understanding Dominant Strategies

A **dominant strategy** is a strategy that produces a better payoff for a player regardless of what another player chooses.

In other words, the player does not necessarily need to predict the other player's decision first. One strategy remains preferable under each possible choice made by the other player.

Imagine two competing companies, Company A and Company B. Each must decide whether to maintain its current advertising budget or increase advertising.

Company A can think through the decision like this:

- If Company B maintains its advertising budget, Company A earns more by increasing advertising.
- If Company B increases advertising, Company A still earns more by increasing advertising.
- Therefore, increasing advertising is Company A's dominant strategy.

If Company B faces the same incentives, increasing advertising would also be its dominant strategy.

A Simple Way to Analyze a Dominant Strategy

When examining a game, you can look at the decision from the perspective of one player at a time.

For Player A, ask:

1. What is my best strategy if Player B chooses Strategy 1?
2. What is my best strategy if Player B chooses Strategy 2?
3. Does the same strategy give me the better payoff in both situations?

If the answer to the third question is yes, we may have identified a dominant strategy.

There are also two variations worth distinguishing.

A **strictly dominant strategy** produces a higher payoff than every alternative strategy regardless of what the other player chooses.

A **weakly dominant strategy** performs at least as well as the alternatives under every possible choice by the other player and performs better under at least one of those choices.

That distinction can become important when two strategies produce equal outcomes under some circumstances.

Not Every Game Has a Dominant Strategy

We should not assume that every strategic problem contains an obvious dominant strategy.

Suppose two restaurants are deciding whether to focus on inexpensive meals or premium dining.

Restaurant A might reason:

- If Restaurant B focuses on premium dining, offering inexpensive meals could help A serve a different segment of the market.
- If Restaurant B focuses on inexpensive meals, Restaurant A might benefit from moving toward premium dining.
- Therefore, Restaurant A's preferred strategy changes depending on Restaurant B's strategy.

In this situation, neither choice is automatically better.

Restaurant A has to consider what Restaurant B is likely to do.

This gives us an important distinction:

Dominant strategy: My preferred strategy stays the same regardless of your choice.

Conditional strategy: My preferred strategy changes depending on your choice.

Many real strategic situations fall into the second category.

Dominant Strategies and Individual Incentives

Dominant strategies also reveal an interesting problem with incentives.

A player can recognize that one outcome would be better for everyone while still having an individual incentive to choose something else.

Imagine two companies that would each earn higher profits if both limited their advertising expenses.

However:

- If Company A limits advertising while Company B advertises aggressively, Company A could lose customers.
- If Company B limits advertising while Company A advertises aggressively, Company B could lose customers.
- Each company therefore has an incentive to advertise aggressively.
- If both advertise aggressively, both companies incur higher expenses.
- Neither company necessarily gains the competitive advantage it was seeking.

The result can look strange from the outside.

Why would both companies choose something that ultimately costs both of them more?

Because the decision facing each individual company is different from the question of what would be best for the companies collectively.

This difference between **individual incentives** and collective outcomes is one of the recurring problems we will encounter throughout game theory.

Game theory does not necessarily tell us which outcome is morally preferable, socially desirable, or best for everyone involved.

It helps us understand the incentives players face and the behavior those incentives can encourage.

Once those individual strategies interact, another question becomes important:

Can the players reach a point where nobody wants to change their strategy alone?

This brings us to Nash Equilibrium.

Nash Equilibrium and Best Responses

A **Nash Equilibrium** occurs when each player's strategy is a best response to the strategies chosen by the other players. At that point, no player can improve their payoff by changing their strategy alone while everyone else's strategy remains unchanged.

The concept is named after mathematician John Nash and has become one of the foundational ideas in modern game theory.

A useful way to understand it is to ask each player a simple question:

"If everyone else continues doing what they are currently doing, would I benefit from changing my strategy?"

If every player answers no, the game is at a Nash Equilibrium.

Understanding a Best Response

A **best response** is the strategy that provides a player with the highest payoff given the strategy selected by another player.

The words "given the strategy" matter.

A best response is not necessarily the strategy a player prefers under every circumstance.

Instead:

- Player B chooses something.
- Player A considers the available responses.

- Player A identifies which response produces the highest payoff.
- That choice becomes Player A's best response to Player B's strategy.

Player B can perform the same analysis in response to Player A.

Where their best responses meet, we may find a Nash Equilibrium.

Example: Two Stores and Evening Hours

Suppose two stores are deciding whether to remain open late.

There may not be enough evening business for both stores to justify the additional operating costs.

Store A might prefer:

- Staying open late if Store B closes early.
- Closing early if Store B stays open late.

Store B faces the same strategic problem.

We could potentially end up with two stable outcomes:

1. Store A stays open late, and Store B closes early.

2. Store B stays open late, and Store A closes early.

Consider the first outcome.

If Store B is closing early, Store A does not want to close because it would lose the evening market.

Meanwhile, if Store A is already serving the evening market, Store B may not want to stay open and incur the additional operating costs.

Neither player benefits from changing alone.

We therefore have a Nash Equilibrium.

The second arrangement could also satisfy the same condition.

This demonstrates another important characteristic of game theory:

A game can have more than one Nash Equilibrium.

Depending on the structure of a game, there may be:

- One equilibrium
- Multiple equilibria
- Equilibria involving different types of strategies

For our purposes, the important point is that Nash Equilibrium is not simply about finding the outcome with the highest numbers.

We are looking for a combination of strategies where each player's choice makes sense given what the others are doing.

A Quick Nash Equilibrium Checklist

When examining a possible equilibrium, ask:

- What strategy has Player A chosen?
- What strategy has Player B chosen?
- Given Player B's choice, would Player A benefit from changing?
- Given Player A's choice, would Player B benefit from changing?
- Can either player improve their payoff by changing alone?

If the answer to the final question is no for every player, we have strong reason to identify the outcome as a Nash Equilibrium.

Equilibrium Does Not Require Players to Know Game Theory

Another important point is that players do not necessarily have to consciously calculate a Nash Equilibrium.

An equilibrium can develop through:

- Experience
- Trial and error
- Observation
- Expectations
- Learning
- Repeated interaction

Imagine two competing businesses repeatedly adjusting their opening hours.

Over time, one discovers that staying open later is profitable while the other discovers that closing earlier works better.

Eventually, neither has much incentive to change.

Their behavior can settle into an equilibrium even if neither business owner has ever heard of Nash Equilibrium.

This becomes particularly interesting once we introduce behavioral economics.

A theoretical model might identify an equilibrium immediately. Real people may take considerably longer to reach it.

They might:

- Misunderstand the strategic situation.
- Have incomplete information.
- Incorrectly predict another player's behavior.
- Experiment with different strategies.
- Copy other players.
- Respond emotionally to previous outcomes.
- Learn from repeated interactions.

This creates a possible gap between a **theoretical equilibrium** and observed behavior.

Behavioral game theory is particularly interested in that gap.

If a model predicts one outcome but people repeatedly choose another, we should investigate why.

Perhaps our assumptions about the players are incomplete.

Perhaps people care about fairness or reputation.

Perhaps the game is difficult to understand.

Perhaps players are making systematic errors.

Nash Equilibrium therefore gives us more than a prediction. It can also provide a benchmark against which actual behavior can be compared.

Why a Stable Outcome Is Not Always the Best Outcome

One of the easiest mistakes to make when learning Nash Equilibrium is assuming that an equilibrium must represent the best possible outcome.

It does not.

A Nash Equilibrium tells us something very specific:

No individual player can improve their payoff by changing their strategy alone while everyone else keeps their strategy unchanged.

That does not mean:

- Everyone is happy.
- Everyone receives the highest possible payoff.
- The outcome is fair.

- The outcome maximizes total welfare.
- The players could not collectively achieve something better.

This distinction is fundamental.

Stability Versus Desirability

Consider two competing businesses that continually spend large amounts of money on promotions.

Both might prefer a situation where they reduce promotional spending and maintain approximately the same market share.

But suppose Company A reduces its spending while Company B continues aggressively promoting.

Company A could lose customers.

The same problem applies to Company B.

As a result:

- Company A continues spending because Company B continues spending.
- Company B continues spending because Company A continues spending.
- Neither wants to reduce spending alone.
- Both continue paying the higher costs.

The situation can therefore be strategically stable while still being financially undesirable for both companies.

This is where another concept becomes useful.

Pareto efficiency describes an outcome where no player can be made better off without making at least one other player worse off.

A Nash Equilibrium does not necessarily have to be Pareto efficient.

That distinction helps us understand why strategic incentives can sometimes produce outcomes that appear inefficient.

You may see this pattern in situations involving:

- Price competition
- Advertising expenditures
- Trade disputes
- Resource use
- Workplace cooperation
- Negotiations
- Arms competition
- Shared responsibilities

Players may recognize that another outcome would be collectively preferable while still lacking an individual incentive to move toward it.

Now Add Human Behavior

Behavioral economics makes the situation even more interesting.

Suppose two players reach an equilibrium that provides reasonably good monetary payoffs, but one person believes the outcome is unfair.

Would that person remain satisfied with the equilibrium?

Maybe not.

If fairness affects that player's preferences, then our original payoff assumptions may be incomplete.

Likewise, someone may willingly accept a smaller immediate monetary payoff because they want to:

- Protect their reputation.
- Punish behavior they consider unfair.
- Reward cooperation.
- Maintain trust.
- Preserve a long-term relationship.

- Encourage future cooperation.

These motivations can change the strategic calculation.

This is why we need to be careful when describing a strategy as "rational."

If we assume a player cares only about money, a particular strategy may appear irrational.

But what if that player values fairness?

What if reputation affects future earnings?

What if today's interaction changes tomorrow's opportunities?

What if the player expects to interact with the same person again?

Suddenly, the payoff becomes more complicated.

A useful distinction to remember is:

Equilibrium asks: Does anyone want to change their strategy alone?

Efficiency asks: Could another outcome make the players collectively better off?

Behavioral analysis asks: Are we accurately describing what the players actually value and how they actually make decisions?

These are related questions, but they are not the same question.

Nash Equilibrium remains extremely useful because it gives us a disciplined way to analyze strategic stability. Behavioral game theory does not replace that framework. It gives us additional ways to understand why observed human behavior may differ from the predictions produced by a simpler model.

And one of the clearest demonstrations of the difference between individual incentives and collective outcomes comes from the Prisoner's Dilemma.

Last Thoughts

Dominant strategies and Nash Equilibrium help us move from identifying the pieces of a game to analyzing what players may actually choose. A dominant strategy remains preferable regardless of another player's decision, while Nash Equilibrium describes a situation in which each player's strategy is a best response to the strategies of others. The important thing to remember is that **strategic stability and collective desirability are not the same thing**. Players can reach an equilibrium that leaves them worse off than another available outcome, and behavioral factors can further change what each player considers valuable. In Chapter 3, we will examine this tension more closely through the Prisoner's Dilemma and explore how competition, cooperation, trust, reciprocity, and fairness affect strategic behavior.

Chapter 3: The Prisoner's Dilemma, Competition, and Cooperation

One of the most interesting problems in game theory occurs when individually attractive choices lead to an outcome that is worse for everyone involved. A player may understand that cooperation could produce a better collective result, yet still have a strong incentive to protect their own interests. When multiple players reason this way, cooperation can break down. The Prisoner's Dilemma provides one of the clearest models of this conflict. More importantly, it gives us a foundation for examining how **trust**, **reciprocity**, and **fairness** influence strategic decisions when real people interact.

Understanding the Prisoner's Dilemma

The Prisoner's Dilemma is a strategic game involving two players who must independently decide whether to cooperate or act in their own immediate interest.

The traditional example involves two suspects who have been arrested and questioned separately. Each prisoner must decide whether to remain silent or confess.

The exact penalties can vary depending on how the game is presented, but imagine the following situation:

- If both remain silent, each receives 1 year in prison.
- If Prisoner A confesses while Prisoner B remains silent, A receives no prison time and B receives 5 years.
- If Prisoner B confesses while Prisoner A remains silent, B receives no prison time and A receives 5 years.
- If both confess, each receives 3 years.

We can organize the possible outcomes like this:

Prisoner A	Prisoner B	A's Outcome	B's Outcome
Remain Silent	Remain Silent	1 year	1 year
Confess	Remain Silent	0 years	5 years
Remain Silent	Confess	5 years	0 years

Confess	Confess	3 years	3 years

Remember that fewer years in prison represent the better payoff in this particular game.

Now consider the problem from Prisoner A's perspective.

If Prisoner B remains silent:

- A can remain silent and receive 1 year.
- A can confess and receive 0 years.
- Confessing produces the better individual outcome.

If Prisoner B confesses:

- A can remain silent and receive 5 years.
- A can confess and receive 3 years.
- Again, confessing produces the better individual outcome.

Prisoner A therefore has a dominant strategy: confess.

Prisoner B faces exactly the same incentives.

The result is:

Both confess and receive 3 years.

But notice what makes the situation interesting.

If both prisoners had remained silent, they would have received only 1 year each.

Collectively, cooperation produces the better outcome.

Individually, however, each prisoner has an incentive to confess.

This creates the dilemma.

Why the Dilemma Matters

The Prisoner's Dilemma demonstrates that individually rational behavior does not necessarily produce the best collective result.

The players are not making obvious mistakes.

Each prisoner can logically explain why confessing makes sense:

- If the other prisoner remains silent, confessing produces the best possible outcome.
- If the other prisoner confesses, confessing protects against the worst possible outcome.
- Therefore, confessing appears preferable regardless of what the other person chooses.

Yet when both players follow this reasoning, both end up worse off than if they had cooperated.

This gives us a useful distinction:

Individual rationality: Choosing the strategy that best protects or advances your own interests given the incentives you face.

Collective rationality: Choosing strategies that produce a better combined outcome for the group.

Those two forms of reasoning do not always point toward the same decision.

The Prisoner's Dilemma Outside of Prison

The model is useful because the underlying structure appears in many economic situations.

Consider two competing businesses deciding whether to begin a price war.

Both companies may prefer to maintain their current prices because higher prices allow both to earn stronger profit margins.

However, each business has an incentive to reduce its price.

If Company A lowers its price while Company B does not, Company A may attract customers away from B.

Company B recognizes this possibility and has the same incentive.

The situation might develop like this:

1. Company A worries that Company B will lower its price.

2. Company B worries that Company A will lower its price.

3. Both reduce prices to protect market share.

4. Neither gains a lasting advantage.

5. Both companies now operate with lower profit margins.

The businesses did not necessarily want the final outcome.

Their incentives pushed them toward it.

Similar structures can appear in:

- Advertising competition
- International trade disputes
- Environmental agreements
- Shared-resource management
- Workplace projects

- Business partnerships
- Negotiations
- Research and development
- Military spending

The details change, but the strategic problem remains similar.

Each player may benefit from mutual cooperation while simultaneously having an incentive to protect themselves from the possibility that the other player will not cooperate.

This is why the Prisoner's Dilemma has become such an important model.

It captures a fundamental problem of strategic interaction:

How can cooperation develop when players have incentives to act in their own immediate interests?

Self-Interest Versus Cooperation

It would be easy to interpret the Prisoner's Dilemma as proof that people are naturally selfish.

That conclusion would be too simplistic.

The model tells us what particular incentives encourage players to do under a specific payoff structure. It does not tell us that people will always behave selfishly in every strategic situation.

In fact, the tension between **self-interest** and cooperation becomes much more complicated when we consider actual human behavior.

Suppose two business partners are working on a project.

Each person has two broad choices:

- Contribute significant effort.
- Contribute minimal effort.

If both contribute significant effort, the project has a strong chance of succeeding.

But each partner may also recognize an opportunity to free ride.

A **free rider** benefits from the efforts of others while contributing relatively little themselves.

One partner might think:

"If the other person is going to work hard anyway, perhaps I can reduce my effort and still benefit from the project's success."

The problem is that the other partner can reason exactly the same way.

If both reduce their effort, the project may fail.

Again, individual incentives can undermine a mutually beneficial outcome.

Why People Cooperate Anyway

If self-interest can create such strong incentives to defect, why does cooperation happen at all?

There are several possible reasons.

People may cooperate because:

- They expect the other player to cooperate.
- They care about the welfare of the other person.
- Cooperation follows an established social norm.
- They want to maintain a positive reputation.
- They expect to interact with the person again.
- They believe cooperation will produce greater long-term benefits.
- They feel an obligation to return cooperative behavior.

- They want to avoid guilt or social disapproval.

This is where behavioral economics becomes particularly important.

A narrow economic model might assume that players care only about their immediate material payoff.

But suppose a player receives psychological satisfaction from behaving fairly.

Or suppose betraying someone creates guilt.

Or perhaps maintaining a reputation for honesty has economic value because other people will be more willing to work with that person later.

In those situations, cooperation may not actually conflict with the player's broader interests.

The definition of the payoff matters.

Cooperation Does Not Mean Ignoring Incentives

We should also avoid the opposite mistake of assuming that cooperation is automatically the superior strategy.

Sometimes competition produces better outcomes.

A company competing aggressively may develop better products, lower prices, or operate more efficiently.

A worker competing for a promotion may develop new skills.

Businesses competing for customers may have stronger incentives to improve service.

The purpose of game theory is not to argue that cooperation is good and competition is bad.

Instead, we should examine the structure of the strategic situation.

Ask:

- What does each player gain from cooperation?
- What does each player gain from competing?
- What happens if one cooperates and the other does not?
- Can a player exploit another player's cooperation?
- Can players observe each other's behavior?
- Will the players interact again?

- Are there consequences for breaking an agreement?

These questions help us determine whether cooperation is strategically sustainable.

The Problem of Unilateral Cooperation

One of the greatest obstacles to cooperation is the possibility of being the only person who cooperates.

Return to the Prisoner's Dilemma.

The worst outcome for a prisoner occurs when that prisoner remains silent while the other confesses.

The fear is not simply:

"I do not want to cooperate."

It may instead be:

"I am willing to cooperate, but I do not want to cooperate if you are going to take advantage of me."

That is a different problem.

And it brings us directly to trust.

Trust, Reciprocity, and Fairness

Traditional game theory gives us the payoff structure of the Prisoner's Dilemma. Behavioral game theory asks what happens when actual people confront strategic situations involving cooperation.

Three behavioral factors become particularly important: trust, reciprocity, and fairness.

Trust

Trust is the willingness to accept some vulnerability based on an expectation about another person's behavior.

In strategic situations, trust can make cooperation possible even when players cannot guarantee what the other person will do.

Imagine two small businesses agreeing to refer customers to one another.

Each business could benefit from the arrangement.

But each also faces uncertainty.

Business A might wonder:

"Will Business B actually send customers to me after I begin sending customers to them?"

Business B may have exactly the same concern.

If neither business trusts the other, the partnership may never develop.

This creates an interesting economic problem.

A potentially valuable transaction can fail even when both players would benefit from successful cooperation.

Trust can therefore have economic value.

It can reduce uncertainty, encourage cooperation, and make transactions possible that otherwise might not occur.

However, trust also creates vulnerability.

A player who trusts indiscriminately can be exploited.

Strategic trust therefore involves evaluating factors such as:

- The other player's past behavior
- Their incentives
- Their reputation
- Whether future interaction is likely
- Whether promises can be verified
- The consequences of betrayal

Trust does not eliminate strategic thinking.

It becomes part of strategic thinking.

Reciprocity

Reciprocity is the tendency to respond to another person's behavior with similar behavior.

People frequently respond positively to cooperation and negatively to perceived exploitation.

For example:

- Someone helps you, so you become more willing to help them.
- A business treats a supplier fairly, and the supplier becomes more willing to accommodate the business later.
- One negotiator makes a reasonable concession, and the other responds with a concession.
- Someone breaks an agreement, and the other player becomes less cooperative.

Reciprocity complicates the assumption that players evaluate every decision independently.

Your decision today may influence how someone treats you tomorrow.

This can change the payoff associated with cooperation.

Suppose cheating another person gives you an immediate gain of $500.

If that action destroys a relationship that could have produced thousands of dollars in future opportunities, the $500 gain may not be strategically attractive.

Likewise, cooperation may produce a smaller immediate payoff while creating larger future benefits.

This is why the time horizon of a game matters.

A one-time interaction and an ongoing relationship can produce very different incentives.

We will examine this more closely when we discuss repeated games in the next chapter.

Fairness

Fairness adds another behavioral dimension.

Traditional models can sometimes treat the size of the material payoff as the primary concern. Actual people may also care about how that payoff is distributed.

Imagine two people receive $1,000 for completing a project together.

One person receives $900.

The other receives $100.

The second person is financially better off than if they received nothing.

But does that mean they will consider the arrangement acceptable?

Not necessarily.

They may compare their payoff with the other person's payoff and conclude that the distribution is unfair.

This introduces the concept of **inequity aversion**, where people experience dissatisfaction from outcomes they perceive as unfairly unequal.

That dissatisfaction can influence strategic behavior.

A person may:

- Reject an unequal offer.
- Refuse future cooperation.
- Punish someone who behaved unfairly.
- Accept a personal cost to prevent another person from benefiting from unfair behavior.
- Reward someone who behaved generously.

From a narrow monetary perspective, some of these choices can look irrational.

From a behavioral perspective, they can make sense if fairness itself is part of what the player values.

The Three Factors Work Together

Trust, reciprocity, and fairness often reinforce one another.

A cooperative relationship might develop like this:

1. Player A takes a small risk and cooperates.
2. Player B interprets the behavior as trustworthy.
3. Player B reciprocates.
4. Both players receive a favorable outcome.
5. Each develops stronger expectations of future cooperation.
6. Continued fair behavior strengthens the relationship.

The opposite pattern can also occur:

1. Player A believes Player B behaved unfairly.
2. Trust decreases.
3. Player A becomes less cooperative.
4. Player B responds negatively.

5. Cooperation deteriorates.

6. Both players may end up worse off.

This helps explain why the history of an interaction can matter as much as the immediate payoff.

People remember.

They develop expectations.

They form reputations.

They adjust their behavior based on previous outcomes.

A simple one-time game cannot always capture those dynamics.

The Prisoner's Dilemma therefore becomes even more interesting when the same players face the decision repeatedly. If today's choice affects tomorrow's behavior, cooperation that appears fragile in a single interaction may become strategically sustainable over time.

Last Thoughts

The Prisoner's Dilemma demonstrates one of the central tensions in game theory: individually attractive strategies can produce collectively inferior outcomes. But behavioral game theory shows us that players do not necessarily evaluate those situations using immediate material payoffs alone. **Trust, reciprocity, fairness, and concerns about exploitation** can influence whether people cooperate, compete, punish, or reward one another. Cooperation is therefore not simply the opposite of self-interest. Under the right conditions, cooperation can become part of a player's broader strategic interest. The next question is what happens when players know they will meet again. In Chapter 4, we will explore repeated games and examine how reputation, rewards, consequences, and future interactions can fundamentally change strategic behavior.

Chapter 4: Repeated Games and Strategic Behavior

Many strategic interactions do not happen only once. Businesses compete with the same companies year after year, coworkers continue working together, countries negotiate repeatedly, and buyers and sellers often develop long-term relationships. When players expect to interact again, the structure of the game can change significantly. A decision that produces the highest payoff today may create consequences tomorrow, while cooperation that seems difficult to maintain in a one-time interaction may become much more attractive when players care about future outcomes. This is the basic idea behind **repeated games**, where the same strategic situation, or a similar one, occurs between players more than once.

What Changes When People Play Again

A **one-shot game** is a strategic interaction that occurs once. Players make their choices, receive their payoffs, and the game ends.

A repeated game is different because previous decisions can influence future decisions.

Consider two businesses that purchase products from each other only once.

Each business might focus heavily on maximizing the immediate value of that single transaction. If one company believes it can gain an advantage without experiencing future consequences, the incentive to do so may be relatively strong.

Now suppose the companies expect to conduct business every month for the next ten years.

The calculation changes.

A company considering taking advantage of the other business now has to consider:

- The profit it could gain today
- The possibility of losing future business
- Damage to its reputation
- How the other company may respond
- Whether cooperation could produce larger long-term benefits
- Whether today's decision changes the other player's future strategy

The immediate payoff has not disappeared. It has simply become one part of a larger strategic problem.

The Shadow of the Future

One useful way to think about repeated interaction is through the **shadow of the future**. This refers to the influence that expected future interactions can have on present behavior.

Suppose cheating another player produces an immediate gain of $1,000.

If the interaction ends immediately afterward, that $1,000 may be highly attractive.

But suppose cheating causes the other player to end a business relationship worth $500 per month for several years.

Now the immediate gain looks very different.

The player has to compare:

Short-term gain versus long-term consequences.

This can create incentives for cooperation that do not exist, or are considerably weaker, in a one-shot game.

The importance of future payoffs can also be represented through a **discount factor**.

In economics, future benefits are often valued less than immediate benefits. A player who strongly values future payoffs may be willing to sacrifice some immediate benefit to maintain a profitable long-term relationship.

A player who cares primarily about the present may behave differently.

For example, imagine two companies could each earn:

- $100,000 by cooperating this year
- An additional $30,000 by exploiting the other company once
- $100,000 per year from continued cooperation afterward

If exploitation causes the relationship to collapse, gaining an additional $30,000 today could destroy several hundred thousand dollars of future value.

A company that places substantial value on future profits may therefore cooperate.

However, a company that believes it will go out of business next month may care much less about preserving the relationship.

The same game can therefore produce different behavior depending on how strongly the players value the future.

Finite and Indefinite Repetition

Not all repeated games have the same structure.

A **finitely repeated game** occurs a known number of times.

For example:

"We will negotiate once per month for the next six months."

An **indefinitely repeated game** does not have a predetermined final interaction. Players know the relationship could continue, but they do not know exactly when it will end.

This distinction can matter.

Suppose two players have successfully cooperated for years but both know with certainty that tomorrow will be their final interaction.

If cooperation was maintained primarily because each player feared future retaliation, that incentive disappears in the final round.

The players may then have an incentive to defect.

But this creates another question.

If both players know they will defect in the final round, what happens in the round immediately before it?

They may recognize that future cooperation will end anyway.

This reasoning can move backward through the game through a process known as **backward induction**.

In some finitely repeated games, this logic can make cooperation difficult to sustain if players are assumed to be perfectly rational and everyone knows exactly when the interaction ends.

Real behavior can differ.

People may continue cooperating because of fairness, habits, social norms, uncertainty, reputation outside the specific game, or because they do not reason backward through every possible future decision.

Once again, behavioral game theory gives us reasons to compare theoretical predictions with what people actually do.

Reputation, Rewards, and Consequences

Repeated interactions allow something that a one-shot game often cannot provide: a history.

Once players can observe previous behavior, they can begin developing expectations about one another.

This gives **reputation** strategic value.

Imagine two suppliers.

Supplier A has repeatedly delivered products on time, honored agreements, corrected mistakes, and communicated clearly.

Supplier B has frequently missed deadlines and attempted to change agreed-upon prices.

A company deciding which supplier to use is unlikely to treat these two businesses as strategically identical.

Their previous behavior provides information about what they may do next.

Reputation therefore becomes part of the strategic environment.

Reputation Can Change the Payoff

Suppose breaking an agreement produces an immediate profit of $10,000.

If there are no future consequences, the player may focus primarily on that gain.

But now suppose breaking the agreement causes:

- The other company to stop doing business with you.

- Future customers to become less willing to trust you.
- Suppliers to demand stronger contractual protections.
- Future negotiations to become more difficult.
- Other players to become less willing to cooperate.

The true payoff from breaking the agreement is no longer simply $10,000.

There are future costs attached to the decision.

This is an important lesson in strategic analysis:

A payoff should reflect the relevant consequences of a strategy, not merely its immediate reward.

Reputation can therefore encourage cooperation even among players primarily concerned with their own economic interests.

Rewards and Punishments

Repeated games also allow players to respond to previous behavior.

Cooperation can be rewarded.

Defection can be punished.

Suppose two businesses agree to share customer referrals.

If Business A consistently sends valuable referrals to Business B, Business B may respond by sending more referrals back.

If Business A stops cooperating, Business B can reduce its own cooperation.

This creates a basic system of strategic consequences:

- Cooperation can lead to continued cooperation.
- Defection can lead to retaliation.
- Returning to cooperation can potentially restore the relationship.

One well-known strategy for repeated interactions is **tit-for-tat**.

The basic version is straightforward:

1. Cooperate initially.
2. Observe the other player's previous action.
3. In the next round, do what the other player did in the previous round.

If the other player cooperates, cooperate.

If the other player defects, defect.

If the other player returns to cooperation, return to cooperation.

The strategy is interesting because it combines cooperation with consequences.

It does not begin aggressively, but it also does not allow repeated exploitation without a response.

However, tit-for-tat is not automatically ideal in every environment.

Suppose Player A accidentally interprets Player B's cooperative action as a defection.

Player A retaliates.

Player B interprets the retaliation as an intentional defection and retaliates in the next round.

Now both players may enter a cycle of retaliation even though neither originally intended to abandon cooperation.

This introduces an important problem: **noise**.

Noise refers to errors, misunderstandings, incomplete observations, or other factors that make it difficult for players to perfectly interpret one another's behavior.

Real strategic interactions contain plenty of noise.

An email is misunderstood.

A shipment arrives late because of circumstances outside the supplier's control.

A competitor changes a price for reasons unrelated to your company.

A coworker misses a deadline because of an emergency.

If every negative outcome is interpreted as intentional defection, cooperation can deteriorate unnecessarily.

Successful repeated interaction may therefore require some degree of forgiveness.

Punishment Must Be Credible

The ability to punish defection can support cooperation, but only if the threatened punishment is believable.

This gives us the concept of a **credible threat**.

Suppose a company tells a supplier:

"If you raise your prices by even one dollar, we will never purchase from you again."

That sounds aggressive.

But suppose the supplier is the only company capable of producing an essential component.

Would the buyer really terminate the relationship over a one-dollar increase?

Probably not.

If carrying out the threat would severely harm the player making it, the other player may recognize that the threat lacks credibility.

Effective strategic consequences therefore depend on whether players actually have an incentive to carry them out.

This is another reason repeated games can become complicated.

Players are not merely responding to actions.

They are evaluating whether promises, threats, and commitments are believable.

Cooperation and Strategy Over Time

Repeated interaction changes cooperation because players can condition their current behavior on what happened previously.

Instead of asking only:

"What gives me the highest payoff right now?"

A player may ask:

"What strategy will produce the best sequence of outcomes over time?"

This shift can make cooperation strategically sustainable.

Conditional Cooperation

Conditional cooperation occurs when a player is willing to cooperate as long as other players also cooperate.

This differs from unconditional cooperation.

An unconditional cooperator might continue cooperating regardless of how the other player behaves.

A conditional cooperator effectively says:

"I am willing to cooperate, but your behavior influences whether I continue."

This type of behavior can make sense in repeated interactions because it balances the benefits of cooperation with protection against exploitation.

Consider two coworkers who regularly share responsibilities.

Their relationship might develop like this:

- Both initially contribute.
- Each observes the other's effort.
- Continued effort strengthens expectations of cooperation.
- If one person repeatedly stops contributing, the other reduces their own effort.
- Cooperation may resume if both return to contributing.

The relationship evolves based on previous behavior.

Strategy Becomes a Pattern

In a repeated game, a strategy is not necessarily a single action.

It can be a rule describing how a player will behave under different circumstances.

For example:

- Always cooperate.
- Always defect.
- Cooperate unless the other player defects.

- Cooperate after cooperation and punish after defection.
- Forgive a single defection but punish repeated defections.
- Cooperate only after observing several rounds of cooperative behavior.

These are strategic patterns.

This matters because repeated games require players to think about both immediate decisions and future responses.

A player may accept a slightly lower payoff today because the action supports a more valuable pattern of cooperation.

Likewise, a player may accept the short-term cost of punishing another player because failing to respond could encourage future exploitation.

Cooperation Can Become Self-Enforcing

One of the most important implications of repeated games is that cooperation does not always require an outside authority to enforce it.

Sometimes the structure of future interaction provides its own enforcement mechanism.

Suppose two businesses earn $50,000 each time they cooperate.

One business could cheat and temporarily earn $70,000.

However, cheating would cause the other business to stop cooperating, reducing future profits to $30,000 per period.

If the companies expect to interact for a long time, the threat of losing future cooperation may be enough to discourage cheating.

In this case, cooperation becomes **self-enforcing**.

The players cooperate because maintaining the relationship serves their interests.

This does not mean contracts, regulations, or formal enforcement are unnecessary in the real world. Those mechanisms can significantly change incentives.

The point is that repeated interaction itself can create strategic reasons to cooperate.

When Cooperation Breaks Down

Repeated interaction does not guarantee cooperation.

Cooperation can become difficult when:

- Players do not expect to interact again.
- Future payoffs are considered unimportant.

- Defection produces extremely large immediate rewards.

- Players cannot observe each other's behavior.

- Misunderstandings occur frequently.

- Punishment is impossible or too costly.

- Players cannot distinguish mistakes from intentional exploitation.

- Trust has already deteriorated.

This helps explain why otherwise productive relationships sometimes collapse.

The problem may not be that cooperation has no value.

The strategic conditions supporting cooperation may have changed.

Imagine two businesses that have cooperated successfully for years. One company suddenly announces that it will leave the market in three months.

The other company may begin behaving differently because the future value of the relationship has declined.

Likewise, if one player believes the other will soon defect, they may decide to defect first.

Expectations can therefore become self-reinforcing.

If I expect you to cooperate, I may cooperate.

My cooperation may encourage you to continue cooperating.

But if I expect you to betray me, I may protect myself by defecting.

My defection may then cause you to defect as well.

The expectation helps produce the behavior that was expected.

What Repeated Games Teach Us

Repeated games give us several important strategic lessons:

- Short-term incentives can differ from long-term incentives.
- Future consequences can make cooperation more attractive.
- Reputation can become an economically valuable asset.
- Players can reward cooperation and punish defection.
- Punishments must be credible to influence behavior.

- Mistakes and misunderstandings can destabilize cooperation.
- Forgiveness can sometimes be strategically useful.
- The probability of future interaction can affect present behavior.
- Cooperation can sometimes become self-enforcing.
- Expectations about future behavior can influence what happens today.

This gives us a much richer picture of strategic decision making.

The question is no longer simply whether cooperation or defection produces the larger immediate payoff.

We also need to consider how today's choice changes tomorrow's game.

And once we begin thinking about behavior across time, human psychology becomes increasingly difficult to separate from strategic analysis.

Last Thoughts

Repeated games show us why the future matters to decisions made in the present. When players expect to interact again, reputation, rewards, retaliation, forgiveness, and the possibility of continued cooperation can become part of the payoff calculation. A strategy that maximizes today's reward may damage a relationship that would have produced substantially greater value over time. At the same time, repeated interaction does not guarantee cooperation. Players still have to manage incentives, uncertainty, mistakes, and the possibility of exploitation. In Chapter 5, we will bring behavioral economics directly into the game theory framework and examine how **bounded rationality, biases, emotions, loss aversion, framing, and social preferences** can change the way people behave in strategic situations.

Chapter 5: Behavioral Economics Meets Game Theory

Traditional game theory provides a structured way to analyze strategic decisions by examining players, strategies, incentives, and expected outcomes. But the usefulness of a model depends partly on how accurately its assumptions describe the people making those decisions. Real players have limited information, limited time, different experiences, and different ways of evaluating risk. They can become emotional, misunderstand other players, rely on shortcuts, or care about outcomes beyond their own monetary payoff. This is where behavioral economics becomes particularly valuable. By combining behavioral economics with game theory, we can examine not only what a player might be expected to do under a particular model, but also why actual behavior may differ from that prediction.

Why People Are Not Perfectly Rational

Traditional economic models often begin with the assumption that people behave rationally. This does not necessarily mean that economists believe people are perfect decision makers. Rationality is an analytical assumption that gives us a consistent framework for predicting choices.

If a player prefers Outcome A to Outcome B, and Outcome B to Outcome C, we generally expect that player to prefer Outcome A to Outcome C.

If one strategy clearly provides a higher payoff without introducing another disadvantage the player cares about, we would generally expect the player to choose it.

These assumptions make economic models manageable.

The problem occurs when we begin treating the assumptions of the model as perfect descriptions of actual human behavior.

People do not always:

- Have complete information.
- Correctly understand the information they possess.
- Evaluate every available strategy.
- Calculate probabilities accurately.
- Anticipate every possible response.
- Maintain consistent preferences.

- Separate emotion from decision making.
- Focus exclusively on monetary outcomes.

This does not mean people behave randomly.

Human behavior can be systematic even when it differs from the predictions of a traditional rational-choice model.

That distinction is important.

Rationality as a Benchmark

Instead of thinking of rationality as a statement about how every person actually behaves, it can be useful to think of it as a **benchmark**.

The model gives us a prediction.

We can then compare observed behavior with that prediction.

Suppose a game predicts that Player A should choose Strategy X because it produces the highest monetary payoff.

But when researchers observe people playing the game, many choose Strategy Y.

We now have an interesting question:

Why?

Perhaps the players misunderstood the game.

Perhaps they evaluated the probabilities differently.

Perhaps Strategy X seemed unfair.

Perhaps they were concerned about how another player would respond.

Perhaps the monetary payoff did not fully represent what they valued.

The difference between predicted and observed behavior becomes something to investigate rather than something to dismiss.

This is an important contribution of behavioral economics.

Preferences Can Be More Complicated Than Money

Consider a negotiation in which you can earn $500 by accepting an agreement.

From a purely monetary perspective, $500 may be better than receiving nothing.

But what if you believe the agreement is intentionally insulting?

What if accepting it damages your reputation?

What if rejecting it sends a message that changes future negotiations?

What if another person receives $50,000 from the same agreement while you receive only $500 despite contributing equally?

The monetary payoff remains $500, but your evaluation of the outcome may change.

This means we need to distinguish between the money attached to an outcome and the player's broader **utility**, or the satisfaction and value the player associates with that outcome.

Utility might be influenced by:

- Money
- Fairness
- Status
- Reputation
- Security
- Risk
- Social approval
- Relationships
- Personal values

This does not mean every game must include every possible human motivation. A model that tries to capture everything may become so complicated that it stops being useful.

Instead, we should ask which motivations are relevant to the strategic problem we are analyzing.

Prediction Versus Explanation

Game theory and behavioral economics can therefore serve complementary purposes.

Game theory may tell us:

"Given these strategies, preferences, and payoffs, this is the predicted outcome."

Behavioral economics can then help us ask:

"Do people actually behave this way?"

And if they do not:

"What behavioral factors might explain the difference?"

This distinction prevents us from turning behavioral economics into a collection of interesting psychological facts.

The behavioral factor matters because it changes how we understand the economic decision.

Bounded Rationality, Biases, and Emotions

One of the most important concepts connecting behavioral economics to strategic decision making is **bounded rationality**.

Bounded rationality recognizes that people attempt to make reasonable decisions while operating under cognitive and informational limitations.

Think about the number of things a perfectly calculating player might need to know in a complicated strategic situation.

The player might need to:

1. Identify every available strategy.
2. Determine every strategy available to the other players.
3. Estimate the probability of each response.
4. Calculate the payoff from every possible outcome.
5. Predict what the other players believe.
6. Consider what those players believe about everyone else.
7. Account for future interactions.

8. Select the strategy that maximizes the desired outcome.

That might be possible in a small game with two players and two strategies.

Now imagine a market containing dozens of competitors, thousands of consumers, uncertain prices, changing regulations, incomplete information, and unpredictable future conditions.

Perfect calculation becomes much more difficult.

People therefore simplify.

Mental Shortcuts

A **heuristic** is a mental shortcut or rule of thumb used to make decisions without analyzing every possible piece of information.

Heuristics can be useful.

A business owner might think:

"When a competitor introduces a major discount, we usually wait a week before responding."

That rule saves the owner from rebuilding an entire strategic model every time a competitor changes prices.

But shortcuts can also produce systematic errors.

These systematic tendencies are commonly called **cognitive biases**.

For strategic decisions, several biases can become particularly important.

Overconfidence bias occurs when people overestimate their knowledge, abilities, or accuracy.

A negotiator may become too confident that the other side will accept an offer.

A business may underestimate a competitor because its executives believe their own strategy is superior.

An investor may believe they can predict how other market participants will react more accurately than they actually can.

Overconfidence matters in game theory because strategic decisions frequently depend on beliefs about other players.

If those beliefs are overly confident, the strategy based on them may be poorly calibrated.

Confirmation bias can create another problem.

People tend to give greater attention to information that supports what they already believe while discounting information that challenges those beliefs.

Suppose a manager believes a competitor is preparing to lower prices.

The manager may pay close attention to every signal supporting that belief while dismissing evidence suggesting the competitor plans to maintain prices.

The company could then respond to a competitive move that was never going to happen.

Emotions Are Part of Strategic Behavior

Emotions can also influence strategic choices.

Imagine someone believes another player intentionally betrayed them.

The player may feel:

- Anger
- Frustration
- Embarrassment
- Distrust
- A desire for retaliation

A purely monetary analysis might suggest that continuing cooperation remains profitable.

But anger may make punishment more attractive.

Likewise, fear can make a player unusually cautious.

Excitement can encourage excessive risk taking.

Regret about a previous decision can affect the next decision.

The behavioral question is not whether emotions are good or bad.

The question is whether they systematically influence strategic behavior.

If they do, they belong in our analysis.

Strategic Mistakes Can Compound

Game theory creates another behavioral challenge because your decision can depend on your beliefs about someone else's decision.

Suppose you incorrectly believe that a competitor will lower prices.

You lower your price first.

The competitor observes your price reduction and concludes that you are starting a price war.

They respond by lowering their price.

Your original prediction was wrong, but your behavior helped make it come true.

The sequence might look like this:

1. You incorrectly predict aggressive behavior.
2. You take defensive action.
3. The other player interprets your action as aggression.
4. They respond aggressively.
5. You interpret their response as confirmation of your original belief.

This type of feedback can make strategic mistakes particularly important.

A mistaken belief does not always remain inside one player's mind.

It can change the game itself.

Loss Aversion, Framing, and Social Preferences

Some behavioral influences become especially important because they affect how players perceive payoffs.

Two objectively similar outcomes may not feel equivalent depending on how they are presented, what the player expected, or how the outcome compares with what other people receive.

Loss Aversion

Loss aversion refers to the tendency for losses to have a stronger psychological impact than equivalent gains.

Suppose you are given two possibilities:

- Gain $1,000.
- Avoid losing $1,000.

Financially, the difference between the two states can be identical depending on the starting point.

Psychologically, they may not feel identical.

People can become particularly motivated to avoid what they perceive as a loss.

This matters strategically because players often evaluate outcomes relative to a **reference point**, such as:

- Their current position
- Their expected outcome
- A previous payoff
- A competitor's performance
- An amount they believe they deserve

Imagine a company currently controls 40 percent of a market.

A competitor enters and threatens to reduce that share to 35 percent.

Management may perceive the change as a loss.

The company might respond much more aggressively than it would if it were entering a new market and deciding whether to increase its share from 30 percent to 35 percent.

The final market share is the same.

The reference point is different.

Loss aversion can therefore affect:

- Negotiations
- Pricing
- Investment decisions
- Competitive responses
- Bargaining
- Risk taking

A player attempting to prevent a loss may accept risks they would not accept when pursuing an equivalent gain.

Framing

Framing occurs when the way a choice is presented influences how the decision is perceived.

Consider these two descriptions:

"Cooperation gives you an 80 percent chance of keeping your current payoff."

"Refusing to cooperate gives you a 20 percent chance of losing part of your current payoff."

The underlying probabilities may describe the same situation.

But the language emphasizes different aspects of the decision.

One emphasizes keeping something.

The other emphasizes losing something.

Framing can influence strategic decisions because players respond not only to objective outcomes but also to how those outcomes are understood.

Negotiators use frames constantly.

A salary proposal might be described as:

"A 5 percent increase."

Or:

"Still 3 percent below the industry average."

Those statements can describe the same salary while creating different reference points.

Strategic players therefore need to consider both the objective payoff and the way the payoff is perceived.

Social Preferences

Earlier we discussed how fairness and reciprocity can affect cooperation. These ideas are part of a broader concept called **social preferences**.

Social preferences describe situations where a person's utility depends partly on outcomes experienced by other people.

This challenges the simplest assumption that players care only about maximizing their own material payoff.

A player may care about:

- Fairness
- Equality
- Reciprocity
- Generosity
- The welfare of others

- Punishing unfair behavior

Consider a simple division of $100.

Player A proposes how the money should be divided.

Player B can accept or reject the proposal.

If B accepts, both receive the proposed amounts.

If B rejects, neither receives anything.

Suppose A proposes:

- $90 for A
- $10 for B

If Player B cared exclusively about receiving as much money as possible, accepting $10 would seem preferable to receiving zero.

But Player B may reject the proposal because the distribution is considered unfair.

At first glance, giving up $10 to receive nothing appears financially irrational.

But suppose Player B receives some utility from punishing unfairness or experiences significant dissatisfaction from accepting an unequal division.

The decision becomes easier to understand.

This does not prove that rejecting the offer is objectively correct.

It demonstrates that our prediction depends on how we specify the player's preferences.

Behavior Can Change the Game We Think We Are Analyzing

This brings us to an important point.

Sometimes observed behavior does not require us to abandon the game theory framework.

Instead, it may require us to reconsider the payoff structure.

Suppose our original model says:

Payoff = Money

But actual players appear to behave as though:

Payoff = Money + Fairness + Reputation + Reciprocity

The strategic structure may remain useful, but our original representation of the player's preferences was incomplete.

In other situations, the issue may be bounded rationality. Players might not correctly identify their best response.

In still other situations, framing or loss aversion may alter how players perceive the available outcomes.

This gives us several possible explanations when behavior differs from a traditional prediction:

- The player values something missing from the original payoff.
- The player has incomplete information.
- The player misunderstands the game.
- A cognitive bias affects the decision.
- Emotion influences the response.
- The player evaluates gains and losses differently.
- The presentation of the choice changes its interpretation.
- The player cares about another person's outcome.

Behavioral game theory asks us to investigate these possibilities rather than immediately labeling unexpected behavior irrational.

At the same time, we should not use behavioral explanations for everything.

If every unexpected decision is explained after the fact by simply naming a bias, the analysis becomes weak.

A useful behavioral explanation should help us understand a consistent pattern of behavior and, ideally, improve our ability to anticipate how people may respond in similar strategic situations.

That is ultimately why behavioral economics strengthens game theory.

It gives us another layer of analysis between the formal structure of a strategic problem and the decisions made by actual people.

Last Thoughts

Behavioral economics does not make game theory obsolete. It helps us examine what happens when the players inside our models behave like actual people. Bounded rationality reminds us that decision makers operate with limited information, time, and cognitive capacity. Cognitive biases and emotions can influence beliefs about other players, while loss aversion and framing can change how outcomes are perceived. Social preferences show that people may also care about fairness, reciprocity, and the welfare of others when evaluating a payoff. The important lesson is not that people are simply irrational. It is that **strategic behavior depends on how players perceive, value, and understand the choices available to**

them. In Chapter 6, we will apply these ideas to business, pricing, competitive strategy, negotiations, and everyday decisions to see how behavioral game theory can help us analyze real strategic situations.

Chapter 6: Behavioral Game Theory in the Real World

Behavioral game theory becomes especially useful when we move beyond controlled examples and apply the framework to decisions people actually face. Businesses must anticipate competitors, negotiators must interpret offers and responses, and individuals routinely make choices whose outcomes depend on what someone else decides to do. These situations rarely contain perfectly informed players making emotionless calculations. Instead, strategic decisions involve incentives, expectations, uncertainty, perceptions, and human behavior. The purpose of behavioral game theory is not to provide a formula that predicts every decision. It gives us a more disciplined way to analyze these interactions while recognizing that the people making the decisions may not behave exactly as a traditional model predicts.

Business, Pricing, and Competitive Strategy

Businesses operate in strategic environments because their decisions rarely occur in isolation.

A company can choose a price, introduce a product, increase advertising, enter a market, or expand production. But the outcome of that decision may depend heavily on how competitors respond.

This makes **competitive strategy** a natural application of behavioral game theory.

Consider pricing.

Suppose Company A is considering reducing the price of a product from $100 to $90.

Management estimates that the lower price will increase sales enough to generate additional profit.

If the analysis ends there, the company has treated the decision almost as though its competitor does not exist.

A strategic analysis asks another question:

What is Company B likely to do after observing the lower price?

Company B could:

- Maintain its existing price.
- Match the $90 price.
- Reduce its price below $90.
- Increase advertising instead.

- Improve the product rather than compete on price.
- Offer a temporary promotion.
- Take no immediate action and observe customer behavior.

Company A's expected payoff from reducing its price depends partly on which response occurs.

If Company B maintains its price, Company A may gain market share.

If Company B matches the reduction, neither company may gain much market share, while both earn lower margins.

If Company B responds even more aggressively, a price war could develop.

This is game theory in practical form.

The Behavioral Side of Competitive Response

Now consider what behavioral economics adds.

Company B is not literally making a decision. People inside Company B are making the decision.

Those managers may be influenced by factors such as:

- Loss aversion
- Overconfidence
- Previous experiences with Company A
- Fear of losing market share
- Internal pressure to respond
- Expectations about Company A's intentions
- How the price reduction is framed within the organization

Suppose Company A intended the price reduction as a temporary attempt to clear excess inventory.

Company B interprets it as an aggressive attempt to capture market share.

Company B responds with a larger price reduction.

Company A then interprets B's response as competitive aggression and reduces prices again.

The result may be a price war neither company originally intended.

The strategic interaction has been shaped by interpretation.

This is an important feature of real competitive behavior.

Players respond not only to what another player does, but also to **what they believe the action means**.

Strategic Signaling

This brings us to **signaling**, where a player's action communicates information that may influence the beliefs or behavior of another player.

A business may:

- Maintain a high price to signal confidence in product quality.
- Make a large investment to signal commitment to a market.
- Publicly announce expansion plans to influence competitors' expectations.
- Offer a generous warranty to signal confidence in reliability.
- Refuse to match a competitor's discount to signal that it does not intend to compete primarily on price.

The important point is that an action can have two effects.

First, it directly changes the player's position.

Second, it may communicate something to other players.

But signals are useful only when other players believe them.

A company can announce that it intends to dominate a market, but competitors do not have to accept the statement at face value.

They can ask:

Does the company have the resources to follow through?

Would carrying out the strategy actually be profitable?

Has the company behaved this way before?

Does the action support the message?

This is similar to the credible threats we discussed in repeated games.

Statements alone do not necessarily change strategic behavior. Players consider whether the incentives behind those statements make them believable.

Market Entry

Market entry provides another useful example.

Suppose a new company is considering entering a market dominated by an established competitor.

The potential entrant might ask:

- How profitable is the market?
- How expensive will entry be?
- How will the existing company respond?
- Will the incumbent lower prices?
- Will it increase advertising?
- Will it introduce competing products?
- Will it tolerate the new entrant?

The incumbent must also think strategically.

An aggressive response might discourage entry.

But aggressive responses can be expensive.

Reducing prices substantially to punish a new competitor may also reduce the incumbent's own profits.

This creates a strategic question:

Is the threatened response actually worth carrying out?

If not, the entrant may decide that the threat is not credible.

Behavioral factors can complicate this calculation.

An established company might respond more aggressively than a narrow profit calculation predicts because executives perceive entry as a loss of territory or status.

An entrant may underestimate the incumbent because of overconfidence.

A history of aggressive competition may cause both companies to expect hostility before either side has actually chosen an aggressive strategy.

Again, the formal incentives matter, but so do the beliefs players bring into the game.

Negotiations and Everyday Strategic Decisions

Negotiation is another clear example of strategic interaction because one person's preferred outcome depends on what another person is willing to accept.

Consider a salary negotiation.

An employee wants a higher salary.

The employer wants to control labor costs while retaining valuable employees.

The employee may know what salary they want but not the maximum amount the employer is willing to offer.

The employer may know its budget but not the minimum amount the employee is willing to accept.

Both sides therefore operate with incomplete information.

The employee might ask:

- How valuable am I to the organization?
- What is the employer likely willing to pay?
- How difficult would I be to replace?
- How credible is my willingness to leave?
- Should I make the first proposal?
- How will the employer interpret my request?

The employer faces its own questions:

- Is the employee likely to leave?
- What would replacement cost?
- Would a raise affect other salary negotiations?
- How much does the employee actually expect?

- Is the employee negotiating or presenting a firm requirement?

Neither side can evaluate its strategy without considering the other.

Anchors and Reference Points

Negotiations also show how behavioral factors can affect strategic outcomes.

An **anchor** is an initial piece of information that influences subsequent judgments.

Suppose a job candidate requests $100,000.

The employer had originally considered offering $85,000.

Even if the employer rejects $100,000, that number may influence the negotiation that follows.

A counteroffer of $92,000 may now appear to be a compromise between two positions.

If the candidate had initially requested $90,000 instead, the negotiation might have developed around a different range.

This does not mean the first number automatically determines the outcome.

The employer still has incentives, information, alternatives, and budget constraints.

But the starting point can affect how later offers are perceived.

Framing can operate similarly.

Consider these statements:

"You would receive a $5,000 increase."

"You would still be earning $5,000 less than comparable employees."

The financial situation can be identical, yet the second statement establishes a different reference point.

The way players perceive an offer can therefore influence whether they accept, reject, or counter it.

Fairness and Negotiation

Fairness becomes particularly important in bargaining.

Imagine two people negotiating how to divide $1,000 from a joint project.

A purely monetary analysis might focus on how much each person can obtain.

Actual negotiation may also involve questions such as:

- Who contributed more work?

- Who took the larger risk?
- What division was originally expected?
- How were similar projects divided previously?
- What do both people consider fair?

A person may reject an economically positive offer because accepting it establishes a precedent they consider harmful.

That may look irrational if we consider only the immediate payment.

It may look more reasonable when we consider future negotiations.

This is another reason strategic decisions should be analyzed within their broader context.

Strategic Interaction Is Everywhere

Formal business negotiations are not the only place these ideas apply.

Strategic interaction occurs whenever your decision depends meaningfully on another person's expected response.

Examples include:

- Deciding how much to offer for a house.

- Choosing whether to negotiate the price of a used car.
- Dividing responsibilities on a group project.
- Deciding whether to share information with a coworker.
- Choosing whether to cooperate with a neighbor.
- Deciding how to respond to someone's concession.
- Determining whether another person's promise is credible.

Even waiting can become strategic.

Suppose two people are deciding who will complete an unpleasant task.

If each person believes the other will eventually do it, both may wait.

The result can be a type of **war of attrition**, where players endure costs while waiting for someone else to give in.

This type of structure appears in much larger economic situations as well, including negotiations, strikes, competitive investment, and disputes.

The scale changes.

The underlying strategic reasoning can remain remarkably similar.

Using Behavioral Game Theory to Make Better Choices

The goal of behavioral game theory is not to turn every decision into a complicated mathematical exercise.

It is also not to teach you how to manipulate other people.

Its practical value comes from improving the questions you ask before making a strategic decision.

When facing a situation involving other players, we can begin with the structure of the game.

Step 1: Identify the Players

Ask:

Who can meaningfully affect the outcome?

Do not automatically assume there are only two players.

A business negotiation might involve:

- A buyer

- A seller
- Competitors
- Suppliers
- Employees
- Regulators
- Customers

Not every participant needs to be included in every model.

The goal is to identify the players whose decisions materially affect the strategic problem.

Step 2: Identify the Available Strategies

What can each important player actually do?

Try to distinguish realistic strategies from theoretically possible but irrelevant actions.

A competitor responding to a price reduction might realistically:

- Match the price.
- Maintain its price.
- Offer a promotion.
- Change its marketing.

- Improve the product.

Listing the available strategies helps prevent us from assuming there is only one possible response.

Step 3: Examine the Payoffs

What does each player gain or lose from the different outcomes?

Money may be important, but it may not be the only relevant payoff.

Consider:

- Profit
- Time
- Risk
- Reputation
- Market share
- Relationships
- Future opportunities
- Fairness
- Security

The purpose is not to invent psychological motives for other people.

It is to avoid assuming that everyone values exactly what you value.

Step 4: Look for Incentives and Best Responses

Now ask:

If I choose this strategy, what would the other player have an incentive to do?

Then reverse the perspective.

If you were the other player, how might you respond?

This can reveal whether your preferred strategy depends on an unrealistic assumption about someone else's behavior.

It can also help identify dominant strategies, best responses, or possible equilibria.

Step 5: Consider the Behavioral Layer

Once the basic strategic structure is clear, consider whether behavioral factors may influence the outcome.

Ask:

- Could loss aversion affect the decision?

- Is someone reacting to a perceived loss rather than an equivalent gain?
- Does fairness matter?
- Is there an important reference point?
- Could overconfidence affect expectations?
- Is the situation being framed in a particular way?
- Does trust influence cooperation?
- Could previous behavior trigger reciprocity?
- Are emotions affecting how actions are interpreted?

This step should come after we understand the underlying strategic problem.

Otherwise, it becomes too easy to explain every decision by simply naming a bias.

Step 6: Consider Time

Ask whether this is truly a one-time interaction.

If the players will meet again, today's strategy can affect tomorrow's payoff.

Consider:

- Reputation
- Future cooperation
- Retaliation
- Rewards
- Learning
- Trust
- Long-term relationships

A strategy that appears profitable in isolation may become unattractive when future consequences are included.

Step 7: Challenge Your Own Assumptions

Perhaps the most useful behavioral lesson is to examine your own reasoning.

Strategic analysis often focuses on predicting someone else.

But you are also a player.

Your own judgment can be affected by the same biases and limitations you are trying to identify in others.

Ask yourself:

- Am I overconfident about what the other player will do?
- Am I interpreting ambiguous behavior as intentional?
- Am I focusing too heavily on avoiding a loss?
- Am I reacting to an anchor?
- Am I assuming the other person values the same things I do?
- Am I ignoring information that contradicts my expectations?
- Am I focusing on today's payoff while overlooking future consequences?

Behavioral game theory becomes considerably more useful when it is applied in both directions.

It helps us think about the other player, but it also helps us examine ourselves.

A Practical Strategic Framework

We can reduce much of the book to a sequence of questions:

1. **Who are the players?**
2. **What strategies are available?**

3. **What are the relevant payoffs?**

4. **What incentives does each player face?**

5. **What are the likely best responses?**

6. **Is there a dominant strategy or likely equilibrium?**

7. **Would cooperation create a better outcome?**

8. **Will the players interact again?**

9. **What behavioral factors could affect the choices?**

10. **What assumptions might I be getting wrong?**

These questions will not eliminate uncertainty.

They are not supposed to.

Strategic decision making frequently involves uncertainty because we cannot completely know what another person will do.

The objective is to organize that uncertainty.

Instead of saying:

"I think they will do this."

We can ask:

"Why would they do this?"

"What incentives support that prediction?"

"What happens if I am wrong?"

"What other responses are plausible?"

That is a much stronger basis for strategic thinking.

Models Are Tools, Not Predictions of Certainty

This brings us back to something important about economics more generally.

A model simplifies reality.

A payoff matrix cannot capture every detail of a business rivalry. Nash Equilibrium cannot tell us everything about a negotiation. The Prisoner's Dilemma does not mean every cooperative problem will end in defection. A behavioral bias does not guarantee that a person will make a particular choice.

These concepts are tools.

They help us isolate important features of a problem and reason about them systematically.

Game theory gives us a framework for understanding strategic interdependence.

Behavioral economics helps us recognize where assumptions about human decision making may need to become more realistic.

Together, they give us behavioral game theory.

The value of that combination is not perfect prediction.

It is **better strategic reasoning**.

Last Thoughts

Behavioral game theory gives us a practical way to examine decisions in business, pricing, competition, negotiation, and everyday life without pretending that human behavior is perfectly predictable. We can identify players, strategies, payoffs, incentives, and possible equilibria while also recognizing that trust, fairness, loss aversion, framing, emotions, expectations, and cognitive limitations can influence what people actually choose. The strongest strategic analysis does not abandon formal game theory for psychology, nor does it ignore human behavior in favor of a perfectly rational model. It uses both. By understanding the structure of the game and the behavior of the people playing it, we can make more informed strategic choices while remaining realistic about the uncertainty involved.

Last Thoughts: Think Strategically, But Remember the Human Side

Game theory gives us a structured way to think about decisions that depend on the choices of other people. Behavioral economics reminds us that the people making those choices do not operate like perfectly predictable machines. Put the two together, and we get a more realistic way to understand strategic behavior. Throughout this book, we have moved from players, strategies, and payoffs to dominant strategies, Nash Equilibrium, the Prisoner's Dilemma, repeated games, and finally the behavioral factors that influence how people actually respond. The concepts are different, but they lead back to the same basic idea: good strategic analysis requires us to understand both the structure of the decision and the people making it.

Look Beyond the "Rational" Choice

One of the most important things to take away from behavioral game theory is that the word "rational" needs to be used carefully.

Traditional economic models give us a valuable starting point. If we know a player's available strategies, preferences, and payoffs, we can analyze which choice should best advance that player's interests.

There is nothing inherently wrong with this approach.

In fact, without some assumptions about rational behavior, strategic analysis would become extremely difficult.

The problem comes when we confuse the assumptions of a model with a complete description of human behavior.

Consider a player who rejects $10 even though accepting the money would leave them financially better off.

If we look only at the monetary payoff, rejecting the offer might appear irrational.

But what if accepting the $10 means allowing another player to keep $990 from something both players contributed equally to?

Now fairness enters the decision.

The player might be willing to sacrifice $10 rather than accept what they consider an extremely unfair outcome.

We can disagree with the decision. We can question whether sacrificing the money is worthwhile. But simply labeling the person irrational does not explain very much.

A better analysis asks:

- What does the player actually value?
- What reference point are they using?
- Does fairness affect their utility?
- Are future interactions important?
- Is reputation involved?
- Does the decision communicate something to the other player?
- Are emotions affecting the response?

Sometimes the answer will still be that the player made a poor decision.

Behavioral economics does not require us to rationalize every choice people make.

People make mistakes.

They misunderstand information.

They become overconfident.

They misjudge probabilities.

They react emotionally.

They rely on shortcuts that sometimes lead them in the wrong direction.

The point is that these behaviors can affect economic outcomes, so they cannot always be ignored.

Start With the Model

A useful approach is to begin with the traditional strategic framework.

Identify:

1. The players.
2. Their available strategies.
3. The relevant payoffs.
4. Their incentives.
5. Their best responses.
6. Possible equilibria.

Then ask whether observed behavior fits the prediction.

If it does, the traditional framework may already explain much of what we need to know.

If it does not, we can investigate further.

Perhaps bounded rationality matters.

Perhaps the payoff structure is incomplete.

Perhaps loss aversion changes how players perceive the outcomes.

Perhaps reciprocity encourages cooperation.

Perhaps an action that looks financially costly today protects a valuable reputation tomorrow.

This approach keeps behavioral analysis disciplined.

We are not simply attaching a psychological explanation to every unexpected outcome.

We are asking whether behavioral factors help explain a meaningful difference between the model and actual behavior.

Rationality Can Depend on the Time Horizon

We should also remember that a decision that looks questionable in the short run can make sense over a longer period.

Suppose a business refuses an opportunity to earn an additional $20,000 because accepting it would require breaking a commitment to a long-term partner.

Looking only at today's payoff, the business appears to have sacrificed $20,000.

But suppose maintaining that relationship is expected to generate $500,000 in future business.

The decision looks very different.

This is why repeated games were so important to our discussion.

Today's payoff is not always the entire payoff.

When strategic relationships continue, reputation, trust, cooperation, and future responses can become economically valuable.

Looking beyond the "rational" choice therefore does not mean rejecting rational analysis.

It means making sure we are analyzing the right choice, the right incentives, and the right time horizon.

Understand the Other Player

Strategic thinking requires a change in perspective.

It is natural to begin a decision by asking:

What do I want?

Game theory requires another question:

What does the other player want?

And then another:

What does the other player think I am going to do?

This is where strategic interaction becomes different from an isolated decision.

Suppose you are negotiating to buy a business.

You have calculated the maximum amount you are willing to pay.

That is useful information, but it does not determine the final outcome.

The seller has their own objectives.

They may care about:

- The selling price
- How quickly the transaction closes
- Whether employees keep their jobs
- Whether they remain involved after the sale
- The certainty of receiving payment
- The reputation of the buyer

- Other offers they expect to receive

If you assume the seller cares only about price, you may misunderstand the game.

Understanding the other player does not mean knowing exactly what they are thinking.

Usually, you cannot.

Instead, strategic reasoning involves identifying incentives and developing reasonable expectations.

Separate Actions From Intentions

Behavioral game theory also teaches us to be cautious about interpreting behavior.

An action and the intention behind that action are not necessarily the same thing.

A competitor lowers its price.

Is it attacking your company?

Maybe.

But perhaps:

- Inventory is too high.
- Demand has weakened.
- Production costs declined.

- The company is running a temporary promotion.
- Management is testing price sensitivity.
- The company is responding to a completely different competitor.

If you immediately interpret the action as aggression, you may respond aggressively.

The competitor may then respond to you.

A strategic conflict can develop partly because of an incorrect assumption about the original action.

This is why good strategic analysis should consider multiple explanations before settling on one.

Ask:

What incentives could reasonably produce the behavior I am observing?

That question is usually more useful than assuming you already know another player's motives.

Think About Their Best Response

One of the most practical habits from game theory is to evaluate your decision from the other player's position.

Before choosing Strategy A, ask:

If I choose A, what becomes attractive to them?

Suppose your strategy works only if the other player responds in a way that clearly harms their own interests.

That should make you question the strategy.

Likewise, if your proposal gives both players a strong reason to maintain cooperation, the arrangement may be more durable.

This is especially important when designing agreements.

A good agreement does not necessarily depend entirely on trust.

It can also align incentives.

If both players benefit from honoring an agreement and both lose from breaking it, cooperation becomes easier to sustain.

That is a stronger strategic position than an agreement where one player continually benefits from defecting and the other simply hopes they will not.

Remember That They Are Analyzing You Too

There is another side to this.

While you are thinking about the other player, they may be thinking about you.

They may ask:

- What does this person really want?
- How far are they willing to negotiate?
- Is their threat credible?
- Will they cooperate?
- Can I trust their promise?
- How will they respond if I change my strategy?

Your behavior therefore becomes information.

Previous actions can influence expectations.

Promises can affect beliefs.

Reputation can change how other players interpret your choices.

This means strategic behavior is not only about responding to the game in front of you.

Sometimes your choices help shape the games you will face later.

Make Better Strategic Decisions

Behavioral game theory cannot tell you exactly what another person will do.

That is an important limitation.

Human behavior is influenced by too many variables for us to reduce every strategic decision to a guaranteed prediction.

What behavioral game theory can do is improve the structure of your reasoning.

Instead of asking only:

"What should I do?"

You can develop a more complete set of questions:

- Who are the relevant players?
- What choices does each player have?
- What does each player value?
- What incentives does each strategy create?
- What are the likely best responses?
- Is there a dominant strategy?
- Where might an equilibrium develop?
- Could cooperation produce a better outcome?

- Can cooperation actually be sustained?
- Will the players interact again?
- What role does reputation play?
- Could behavioral factors change the expected response?
- What happens if my prediction is wrong?

That final question deserves particular attention.

Think in Scenarios, Not Certainties

Suppose you believe a competitor has a 70 percent chance of maintaining its current price and a 30 percent chance of reducing it.

You do not know what the competitor will do.

But you have moved beyond a vague prediction.

You can now consider both possibilities.

If they maintain the price, what should you do?

If they reduce it, what should you do?

How costly would it be if your expectation is wrong?

Can you choose a strategy that performs reasonably well under both scenarios?

Strategic thinking often becomes stronger when we stop trying to predict one future with certainty and instead examine several plausible responses.

Know When Cooperation Changes the Game

Another important lesson from this book is that competition is not always the only strategic possibility.

Sometimes players can create value through cooperation.

The important question is whether that cooperation can survive the incentives each player faces.

Look for conditions that support it:

- Future interaction
- Mutual benefits
- Observable behavior
- Reputation
- Credible consequences
- Reciprocity
- Trust
- Aligned incentives

Then look for conditions that threaten it:

- Large rewards for defection
- Little chance of future interaction
- Poor information
- Weak accountability
- Frequent misunderstandings
- Unbalanced benefits
- Loss of trust

This approach gives us a more realistic understanding of cooperation.

Cooperation does not have to depend on everyone being generous.

Sometimes cooperation survives because it is strategically valuable.

Remember Your Own Behavioral Limits

Finally, do not make the mistake of using behavioral economics only to analyze other people.

You are a player too.

You can be overconfident.

You can anchor on the first number you hear.

You can become overly focused on avoiding a loss.

You can interpret another player's behavior emotionally.

You can search for evidence supporting what you already believe.

You can underestimate uncertainty.

In some situations, recognizing your own behavioral tendencies may be more valuable than identifying someone else's.

Before making an important strategic choice, it can therefore help to ask:

Am I analyzing the game, or am I reacting to it?

That question does not mean emotion should be removed from every decision. Nor does it mean intuition has no value.

It means we should understand what is influencing the choice.

That awareness gives us an opportunity to reconsider assumptions before acting on them.

Game theory gives us the structure.

Behavioral economics gives us a more realistic understanding of the player.

Behavioral game theory brings the two together.

Last Thoughts

The central lesson of behavioral game theory is not that people are irrational, nor is it that traditional game theory fails because human behavior is complicated. The more useful conclusion is that **strategic decisions have both a structural and a behavioral side**. Players respond to incentives, but they also interpret those incentives through expectations, experiences, emotions, biases, social preferences, and beliefs about other people. Good strategic thinking requires us to consider both. Understand the game, understand the incentives, think carefully about the other players, and remain aware of the assumptions shaping your own decisions. You will not always predict what another person will do, but you can become much better at understanding the strategic situation in which the decision is being made.

About the Author

Roggie "Raj" Clark is an entrepreneur and a 10-year marketing professional with a proven track record in e-commerce and digital business growth. Having built and managed successful online stores with thousands of sales and consulted for numerous marketing clients, Roggie has mastered the intricacies of online marketing, branding, and consumer behavior. He has also written several popular books on digital marketing, SEO (search engine optimization), and programming (HTML, CSS, and JavaScript).

As a former marketing manager at a fintech company—a role he secured through his own marketing and financial expertise—Roggie gained firsthand experience in financial strategy and wealth-building. This journey inspired him to share insights with amateur investors, helping them save money, make smarter financial decisions, and build long-term wealth. Raj currently lives in Maryland with his sister and niece.

www.ingramcontent.com/pod-product-compliance
Lightning Source LLC
LaVergne TN
LVHW050821061126
851857LV00012B/910
9798240825170